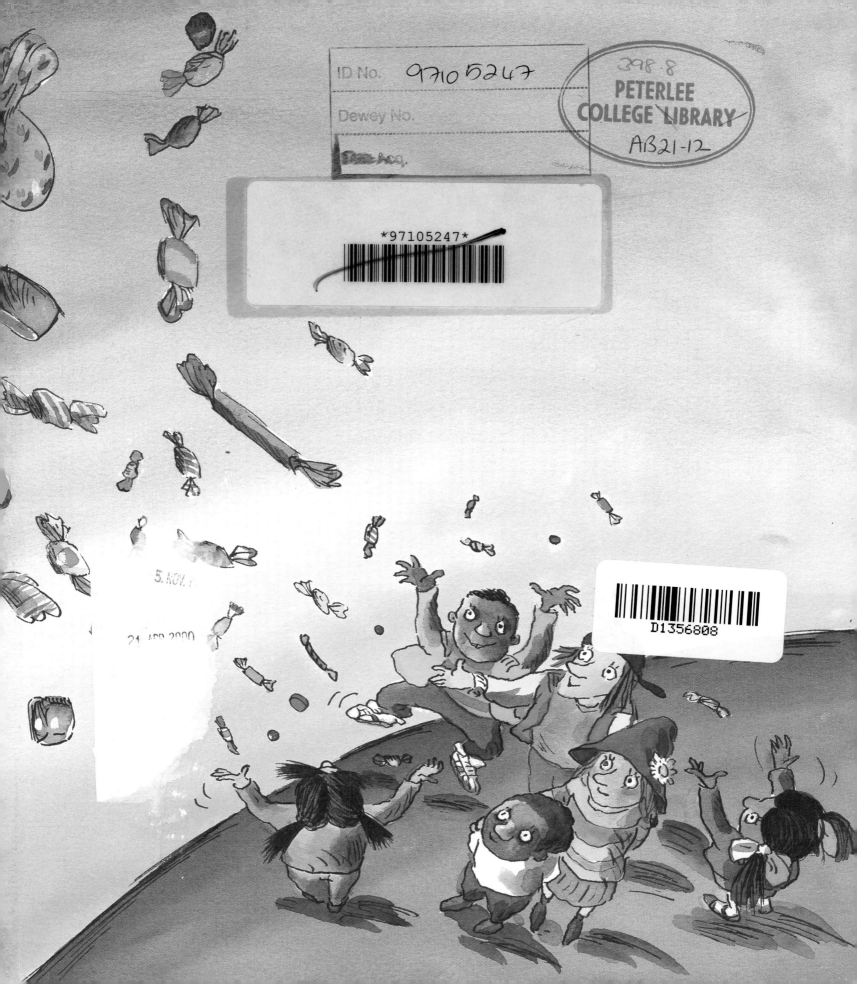

Oxford University Press, Walton Street, Oxford OX2 6DP

Oxford New York Toronto
Delhi Bombay Calcutta Madras Karachi
Petaling Jaya Singapore Hong Kong Tokyo
Nairobi Dar es Salaam Cape Town
Melbourne Auckland

and associated companies in
Berlin Ibadan

Oxford is a trade mark of Oxford University Press

A CIP catalogue record for this book is
available from the British Library

ISBN 0 19 276092 0

Typeset by FWT Studios
Printed in Hong Kong

Twinkle Twinkle Chocolate Bar

Rhymes for the very young

Compiled by John Foster

Oxford University Press

Oxford   New York   Toronto

Acknowledgements

Dorothy Aldis, 'Ice' reprinted by permission of G. P. Putnam's Sons from *Everything and Anything*, copyright 1925-1927, copyright renewed 1953-1955 by Dorothy Aldis. **Jonathan Allen**, 'The Underwater Camel' from *A Bad Case of Animal Nonsense*. Reprinted by permission of J. M. Dent & Sons Ltd Publishers. **David Andrews**, 'The Picallili Monster'. Reprinted by permission of the author. **Leila Berg**, 'Swinging' and 'A Garden' from *Time For One More* (Methuen Children's Books). Reprinted by permission of Octopus Publishing Group. **Valerie Bloom**, 'Clouds' and 'Water Everywhere'. © 1991 Valerie Bloom. Reprinted by permission of the author. **Ann Bonner**, 'Mud' © 1991 Ann Bonner. Reprinted by permission of the author. **Tony Bradman**, 'Bath-Time' *A Kiss On The Nose* (William Heinemann Ltd). Reprinted by permission of Octopus Publishing Group. 'The Sandwich', © 1991 Tony Bradman. Reprinted by permission of the author and Rogers Coleridge & White. **Dave Calder**, 'This is the key to the castle'. © Dave Calder from *Bamboozled* (Other Pubns, 1987). Reprinted by permission of the author. **Charles Causley**, 'Charity Chadder' from *Early in the Morning* (Puffin). Reprinted by permission of David Higham Associates Ltd. **John Coldwell**, 'My sister's eating porridge', © 1991 John Coldwell. Reprinted by permission of the author. **Wendy Cope**, 'Telling' and 'My Old Guitar' from *Twiddling Your Thumbs*. Reprinted by permission of Faber & Faber Ltd. **Sue Cowling**, 'Silly Question', published in *What Is a Kumquat?* (Faber, Spring 1991). Reprinted by permission of the author and publisher. **John Cunliffe** 'Soggy Greens' and 'Humpty Dumpty' both © 1991 John Cunliffe. Reprinted by permission of David Higham Associates Ltd. **Olive Dove** 'How Far', first published in *Poetry Corner*, BBC, Spring 1981. Reprinted by permission of the author. **Richard Edwards**, 'Dorothy Porridge', © 1991 Richard Edwards. Reprinted by permission of the author. **Eric Finney**, 'Gone' © 1991 Eric Finney. Reprinted by permission of the author. **Aileen Fisher**, 'After a Bath' from *Up The Windy Hill*. Copyright 1953 by Aileen Fisher, copyright renewed 1981. Reprinted by permission of the author. **John Foster**, 'Where are you going, Johnny?', 'When the Wind Blows' and 'Sitting in my bath tub', all © 1991 John Foster. Reprinted by permission of the author. **Rose Fyleman**, 'Tadpoles'. Reprinted by permission of The Society of Authors as the literary representative of the Estate of Rose Fyleman. **Robert Heidbreder**, 'A Big Bare Bear' from *Don't Eat Spiders*, poems © Robert Heidbreder 1985. Reprinted by permission of Oxford University Press Canada. **Theresa Heine**, 'Painting Faces' and 'Who Is It?', both first appeared in *A Big Poetry Book* (Basil Blackwell, 1989), 'My Brother' and 'Jack Frost' are both © 1991 Theresa Heine. All poems are reprinted by permission of the author. **Maggie Holmes**, 'Hair Drier', © 1991 Maggie Holmes. Reprinted by permission of the author. **John Kitching**, 'Lost and Found', 'I Like Cabbage', 'Fish and Chips', 'One, Two', 'Don't', 'My Bike' and 'Bed-Time'. All © 1991 John Kitching. Reprinted by permission of the author. **Mary Jefferies**, 'Snow-lady', © 1991 Mary Jefferies. Reprinted by permission of the author. **John Jenkins**, 'Juniper Jim' from *More Stuff and Nonsense*, ed. Michael Dugan (Collins/Angus & Robertson Publishers). Copyright John Jenkins. Reprinted by permission of the author. **Diana Harland**, 'Jane', reprinted in *Allsorts 2*, edited by Ann Thwaite (Macmillan 1969). **Jean Kenward**, 'Giant Thunderclogs', © 1991 Jean Kenward. Reprinted by permission of the author. **Dennis Lee**, 'Mrs Magee', 'The Snowstorm', 'Silverly' and 'Good Night, Good Night' all from *Jelly Belly*. © Dennis Lee. Reprinted by permission of McKnight, Gosewich Associates Agency Inc. **Valerie McCarthy**, 'Caspar the Cat', reprinted from *Nursery Rhymes and Songs From Listen With Mother* (BBC). **Ian McMillan**, 'Going to Sleep', © 1991 Ian McMillan. Reprinted by permission of the author. **Spike Milligan** 'Polar Bear', reprinted in *Startling Verse For All the Family*. Reprinted by permission of Spike Milligan Productions Ltd. **Trevor Millum**, 'Valerie Malory and Sue Hu Nu'. © 1991 Trevor Millum. Reprinted by permission of the author. **Cynthia Mitchell**, 'A Frog and a Flea' reprinted from *Hallowe'en Hecate* (William Heinemann Ltd.). **Pamela Mordecai**, 'Caribbean Counting Rhyme', first published in *Sunjet*, Air Jamaica's flight magazine. Reprinted by permission of the author. **David R. Morgan**, 'Where's Melissa?', © 1991 David R. Morgan. Reprinted by permission of the author. **Brian Moses**, 'Granny Goat', 'Magic Shoes', © 1991 Brian Moses. Reprinted by permission of the author. **Judith Nicholls**, 'Sounds Good' first published in *Higgledy-Humbug* (Mary Glasgow Publications), 'Toes', © 1991 Judith Nicholls. Both published by permission of the author. **Janet Paisley**, 'The Mud-pie Makers Rhyme', and 'Fancy Me', both © 1991 Janet Paisley. Reprinted by permission of the author. **Al Pittman**, 'Roger was a Razor Fish'. Reprinted by permission of Breakwater. **Kjartan Poskitt**, 'The Moon' *Pob and Friends*, ed. Anne Wood. Reprinted by permission of the author and Ragdoll Productions. **Joan Poulson**, 'Tea-Time Treat', 'Like an Animal', 'A dibble-dubble day' and 'Patchy Bear', all © 1991 Joan Poulson. Reprinted by permission of the author. **Jack Prelutsky**, 'Dora Diller' from *The New Kid on the Block*. © 1984 by Jack Prelutsky. Reprinted by permission of Greenwillow Books, William Morrow & Co., Inc. and William Heinemann Ltd. **John Rice**, 'Gogo Cat' and 'Dog Talk', both © 1991 John Rice. Reprinted by permission of the author. **Clive Riche**, 'The Wobbling Race', © 1991 Clive Riche. Reprinted by permission of the author. **Paul Rogers**, 'Undertable Land', © 1991 Paul Rogers. Reprinted by permission of the author. **Michael Rosen**, 'On the Beach' from *Smelly Jelly Smelly Fish: The Seaside Book*, text © 1986 Michael Rosen, illustrations © 1986 Quentin Blake. 'Messing About' ('Fooling Around') from *Under the Bed*, text © 1986 Michael Rosen, illustrations © 1986 Quentin Blake. Reprinted by permission of the publishers, Prentice Hall Books for Young Readers/A trademark of Simon & Schuster, Inc. N.Y. 10020, and Walker Books Limited, London. **Charles Thomson**, 'My Friend Camilla' and 'Over the Park' both © 1991 Charles Thomson. Reprinted by permission of the author. **Barrie Wade**, 'Lullaby', © 1991 Barrie Wade. Reprinted by permission of the author. **John Walsh**, 'Danger Game', this version © 1991 John Walsh. Reprinted by permission of the author. **Dave Ward**, 'Run, Run', © 1991 Dave Ward. Reprinted by permission of the author. **Clyde Watson**, 'Here is the Nose' and 'Storm' ('Jagged light, blue and bright'), from *Catch Me and Kiss Me and Say It Again* (Collins/Philomel). Text © 1976, 1978 by Clyde Watson. Reprinted by permission of Curtis Brown Ltd. and Philomel Books. **Clive Webster**, 'Giant', 'The Fiery Dragon', 'Jungle Wedding' and 'The Sunshine Tree', all © 1991 Clive Webster. Reprinted by permission of Clive Webster. **Colin West**, 'An Alphabet of Horrible Habits' from *It's Funny When You Look At It*, and 'Farmer's Shadow' from *A Moment In Rhyme*. Both reprinted by permission of the Random Century Group Limited.

Although every effort has been made to secure copyright permission prior to publication, in a few instances this has not been possible. If notified, the publisher will be pleased to rectify any errors or omissions at the earliest opportunity.

Illustrations are by: **Ian Beck** pp. 76-77, 94-95; **Christine Blaney** pp. 34-35, 74-75; **Bucket** pp. 12-13, 24-25, 40-41, 48-49; **Jane Gedye** pp. 28-29, 82-83, 92-93; **David Holmes** pp. 66-67, 68-69; **Norman Johnson** pp. 10-11, 26-27; **Thelma Lambert** pp. 20-21, 36-37, 62-63; **Vanessa Luff** pp. 18-19; **Valerie McBride** pp. 70-71; **Isobel Morgan-Giles** pp. 32-33, 38-39; **Rosemary Murphy** pp. 80-81; **Jenny Norton** pp. 60-61; **Korky Paul** pp. 52-53, 54-55; **Tony Ross** pp. 4-5, 6-7, 8-9; **Nick Sharratt** pp. 14-15, 58-59; **Denise Teasdale** pp. 16-17, 90-91; **Pamela Venus** pp. 22-23, 44-45, 46-47, 88-89; **Gini Wade** pp. 50-51; **Brian Walker** pp. 42-43, 72-73; **Jocelyn Wild** pp. 56-57, 86-87, 98-99; **Brian Wildsmith** 30-31, 96-97; **Jenny Williams** pp. 64-65, 78-79, 84-85.

Jacket and endpaper illustrations: **Tony Ross**

Contents

Twinkle Twinkle Chocolate Bar

Twinkle twinkle chocolate bar
Your dad drives a rusty car
Press the starter
Pull the choke
Off he goes in a cloud of smoke.

Anon

On the Beach

There's a man over there
and he's sitting in the sand.
He buried himself at tea-time,
now he's looking for his hand.

There's a boy over there
and he's sitting on the rocks,
eating apple crumble,
washing dirty socks.

There's a woman over there
sitting in the sea,
I can see her
but she can't see me.

There's a girl over there
and she's sitting on a chair.
Standing just behind her
is a big grizzly bear.

Michael Rosen

Messing About

'Do you know what?'
said Jumping John.
'I had a bellyache
and now it's gone.'

'Do you know what?'
said Kicking Kirsty.
'All this jumping
has made me thirsty.'

'Do you know what?'
said Mad Mickey.
'I sat in some glue
and I feel all sticky.'

'Do you know what?'
said Fat Fred.
'You can't see me,
I'm under the bed.'

Michael Rosen

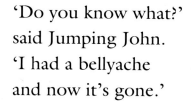

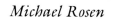

Danger Game

Jessica was playing
On the escalator.
When suddenly she tripped
And the escalator ate her!

John Walsh

Dora Diller

'My stomach's full of butterflies!'
lamented Dora Diller.
Her mother sighed. 'That's no surprise,
you ate a caterpillar!'

Jack Prelutsky

Lost and Found

Jonathan Randall
Lost his sandal;
Couldn't find it
With torch or candle.

Kirsty Cox
Lost her socks;
Found them
In the cornflakes box.

John Kitching

Silly Question

'Why is your pram full of holly?
There should be a baby inside.'

'My baby is watching the telly,
And the holly's enjoying the ride.'

Sue Cowling

Mrs Magee

Mrs Magee
Climbed into a tree,
And she only came down to go shopping.
A branch was her bed,
With a leaf on her head —
And whenever it rained, she got sopping.

Dennis Lee

Charity Chadder

Charity Chadder
Borrowed a ladder,
Leaned it against the moon,
Climbed to the top
Without a stop
On the 31st of June,
Brought down every single star,
Kept them all in a pickle jar.

Charles Causley

14

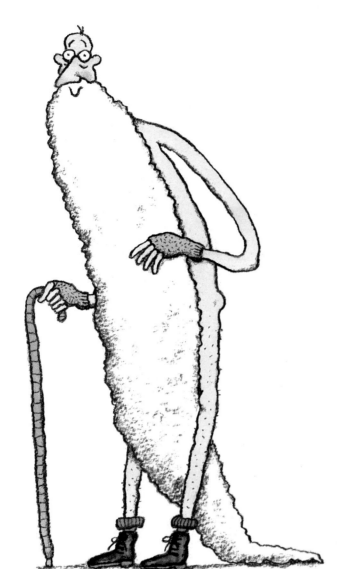

Dorothy Porridge

Dorothy Porridge is wearing a lettuce
And nobody quite knows why,
She's racing around like the spin of a coin
And waving her fist at the sky.
The last time I saw her she lifted a leaf
And gave me a wink of her eye,
Dorothy Porridge is wearing a lettuce
And nobody quite knows why.

Richard Edwards

Juniper Jim

Juniper Jim
Is very thin
As well as very old,
And if it wasn't for
The length of his beard
He would catch his death of cold.

John Jenkins

Gogo Cat

Gogo cat has an orange coat
    He also wears black wellies,
He lost his thermal underwear
    So now he borrows Nelly's.

Gogo cat has a bath each night
    He dives into the basin,
We keep a saucer full of milk
    For him to wash his face in.

John Rice

Caspar the Cat

Caspar the cat,
Lives in a flat,
And he hates to get his fur soggy.
When he's caught in a shower,
He turns very sour,
And then he's a bad-tempered moggy!

Valerie McCarthy

Dog Talk

Pebbles and shells
Water down wells
Churches and bells
Your dog smells.

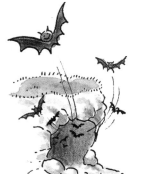

Sand and waves
Bats and caves
Rants and raves
My dog behaves.

Beetles and slugs
Fleas and rugs
Kisses and hugs
Your dog's got bugs.

Keys and locks
Feet and socks
Eagles and hawks
My dog talks!

John Rice

17

Granny Goat

Eat anything
will granny goat,
handkerchiefs,
the sleeve of your coat,
sandwiches,
a ten pound note,
eat anything
will granny goat.

Granny goat
goes anywhere,
into the house
if you're not there,
follows you round,
doesn't care,
granny goat
goes anywhere.

Granny goat
will not stay
tied up
throughout the day,
chews the rope,
wants to play,
granny goat
won't stay

anywhere you
want her to,
she would rather be
with YOU!

Brian Moses

Soggy Greens

Oh soggy greens, I hate you,
I hate your sloppy slush;
And if my mum would let me,
I'd throw you in a bush.

Oh apple pie, I love you,
I love your crunchy crust;
And if my mum would let me,
I'd eat you till I bust.

John Cunliffe

I Like Cabbage

I like eating cabbage,
Turnip, beetroot, cress,
Very smelly foreign cheese
And, best, (you'll never guess)
It isn't chocolate or ice-cream,
No, no, it isn't custard,
My very best, my favourite food,
Is sausages with mustard.

John Kitching

21

Sounds Good!

Sausage sizzles,
crispbreads crack;
hot dogs hiss
and flapjacks snap!

Bacon boils
and fritters fry;
apples squelch
in apple pie.

Baked beans bubble,
gravy grumbles;
popcorn pops,
and stomach rumbles. . .

I'M HUNGRY!

Judith Nicholls

Fish and Chips

Fish and chips,
Fish and chips.

Greasy fingers,
Greasy lips.

Eat too many
Get fat hips.

I don't care.
  — More fish and chips!

John Kitching

Tea-time Treat

John likes jam.

His mother said
'Don't put so much
upon your bread.'

So instead,
he spread it thickly
on his head.

Joan Poulson

23

The Sandwich

Oh what shall I have
    Today for my tea?
I know — a sandwich,
    As big as can be!

I'll start with the bread,
    Two slices, quite large;
Then slap on some jam,
    Oh yes, and some marge,

I'll put in some cheese,
    A tomato or two,
And maybe an onion
    This big one will do!

I'll bung in some lettuce,
    A radish, of course,
And . . . a sizzling burger,
    All covered in sauce!

24

Add in some chicken,
    And maybe some chips,
Some biscuits, an apple,
    A packet of crisps,

A cake with some candles,
    Some chocolate (one bar),
Spaghetti, bananas,
    Sweets from a jar,

Baked beans and humbugs,
    Carrots and mustard,
All topped off with cream
    And steaming hot custard . . .

Now a sandwich like that
    You really can't beat,
It's packed out with goodies,
    A real tasty treat.

There's only one problem;
    It's breaking my heart . . .
It's such a big sandwich –
    Where do I start?

Tony Bradman

My Sister's Eating Porridge

My sister's eating porridge
It's going everywhere.
Up her nose and down her front;
A dollop in her hair.

My sister's eating porridge,
She's missed her mouth again.
Now it's dripping off her spoon
Like lumpy porridge rain.

My sister's eating porridge
And most is on the floor.
No wonder she is hungry
And crying out for, 'More!'

John Coldwell

Humpty Dumpty

Humpty Dumpty
Sat on the wall,
Eating a big
Ice-cream.
He dropped a blob
Down Mary's back,
And she began
To scream.

John Cunliffe

27

The Wobbling Race

Two jellies had a wobbling race
To see who was the wibbliest.
Then the sun came out and melted them
And made them both the dribbliest.

Clive Riche

A Frog and a Flea

A frog and a flea
And a kangaroo
Once jumped for a prize
In a pot of glue;
The kangaroo stuck
And so did the flea,
And the frog limped home
With a fractured knee.

Cynthia Mitchell

Valerie Malory & Sue Hu Nu

Valerie Malory and Sue Hu Nu
Went to school on a kangaroo
Half way there and half way back
They met a duck with half a quack.

Valerie Malory and Sue Hu Nu
Arrived at school with a kangaroo
Half way there and half way in
They met a cat with half a grin.

Valerie Malory and Sue Hu Nu
Came home from school on a kangaroo
Half way here and half way there
They met a clown with half a chair.

Valerie Malory and Sue Hu Nu
Went upstairs on a kangaroo
Half way up and half way down
They met a king with half a crown.

Valerie Malory and Sue Hu Nu
Went to bed with a kangaroo
Half asleep and half awake
They dreamt of a . . . duck and a quack
  and a grin and a cat
    and a king and a clown
      and a chair and a crown
        and a kangaroo
          with half a shoe.

Trevor Millum

An Alphabet of Horrible Habits

A is for Albert who makes lots of noise

B is for Bertha who bullies the boys

C is for Cuthbert who teases the cat

D is for Dilys whose singing is flat

E is for Enid who's never on time

F is for Freddy who's covered in slime

G is for Gilbert who never says thanks

H is for Hannah who plans to rob banks

I is for Ivy who slams the front door

J is for Jacob whose jokes are a bore

K is for Kenneth who won't wash his face

L is for Lucy who cheats in a race

M is for Maurice who gobbles his food

N is for Nora who runs about nude
O is for Olive who treads on your toes
P is for Percy who *will* pick his nose
Q is for Queenie who won't tell the truth
R is for Rupert who's rather uncouth
S is for Sibyl who bellows and bawls
T is for Thomas who scribbles on walls
U is for Una who fidgets too much
V is for Victor who talks double Dutch
W is for Wilma who won't wipe her feet
X is for Xerxes who never is neat
Y is for Yorick who's vain as can be
And Z is for Zoe who doesn't love me

Colin West

Painting Faces

Funny faces,
Fat and thin,
Have you put the eyebrows in?
Noses pointed, lips are blue,
This one looks a bit like you.

Theresa Heine

Jane

Jane's been drawing on the wall,
Naughty little Jane.
And now she's trying very hard
To lick it off again.

Diana Harland

Who is it?

Take . . .
    A head, some shoulders, knees, and toes,
    A mouth and eyes that see,
    A pair of legs, two feet, one nose,
    And what you've got is
                ME!

Theresa Heine

Undertable Land

Daddy's baggy trousers,
Grandma's bony knees,
Tommy's lost a slipper,
Someone's dropped some cheese.

Chair legs, their legs, table legs,
The hairs on Grandpa's hand . . .
No one knows what I can see
In Undertable Land.

Up above the table top,
Chatter and clatter of tea.
Down here, invisible,
No one else but me.

Listening to what they say . . .
Some I understand.
But I know all there is to know
In Undertable Land.

Paul Rogers

Giant

I come up to
My brother's knee.
But that's because
I'm only three.

But when I'm four
I will be able
To see what's on
The kitchen table.

And when I'm five
I know that I
Will be so big
I'll reach the sky.

Clive Webster

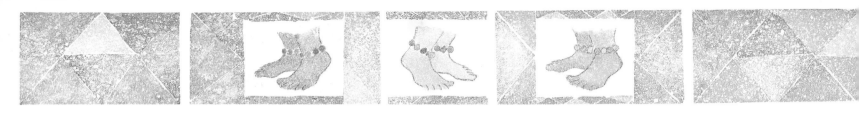

Toes

Toes,
handy to wiggle,
useful to kick;
fun to tickle,
hard to lick!
Good to count on,
walk on, run —
feet without toes
would be much less fun!
To me it's quite clear
there is nothing as neat
as a fine set of toes
on the end of your feet!

Judith Nicholls

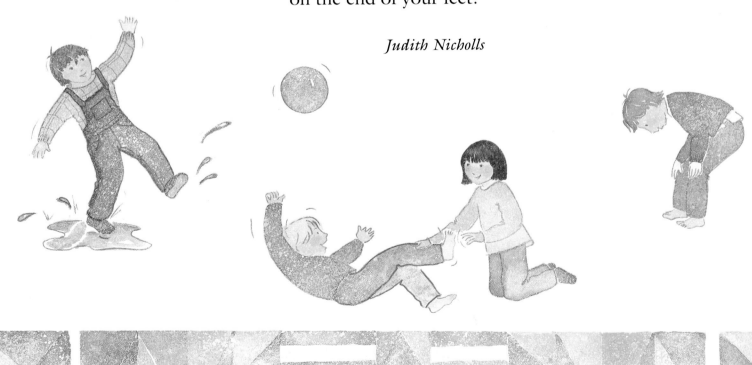

Telling

One, two, three, four,
Telling Miss that Gary swore.
Five, six, seven, eight,
Now I haven't got a mate.

Wendy Cope

One, Two

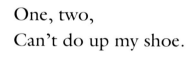

One, two,
Can't do up my shoe.

Three, four,
Drop my food on the floor.

Five, six,
Give my plate greedy licks.

Seven, eight,
Get to school late.

Nine, ten,
Mum won't tell me again.

John Kitching

Run, Run!

Run, Run —
Here comes Mum,
She's got porridge in her hair.

Run, Run —
Here comes Mum,
She's found the spider on her chair.

Run, Run —
Here comes Mum,
And she knows who put it there!

Dave Ward

Don't

Don't do this, don't do that.
Don't scrape your plate.
Don't tease the cat.
Don't pick your nose.
Don't suck your thumb.
Don't scratch your head.
Don't swallow gum.
Don't stick your tongue out.
Don't make that face at me.
Don't wear your socks in bed.
Don't slurp your tea.
Don't touch your father's records.
Don't touch your brother's glue.

So many things I *mustn't* —
Whatever *can* I do?

John Kitching

40

My Brother

He giggles and squeaks,
And curls and rolls,
And wriggles and cries,
And screws up his eyes,
And squirms and squeals,
And shouts and yells,
And screeches and begs,
And kicks his legs,
Till Mum puts her head
Round the door and says
'Stop tickling your brother!'

Theresa Heine

Here is the Nose

Here is the Nose that smelled something sweet
And led the search for a bite to eat.

Here are the Feet that followed the Nose
Around the kitchen on ten Tiptoes.

Here are the Eyes that looked high and low
Till they spotted six pans sitting all in a row.

Here are the Arms that reached up high
To bring down a fresh-baked blueberry pie.

Here is the Mouth that opened up wide.
Here are the Hands that put pie inside.

Here is the Tongue that licked the tin
And lapped up the juice running down the Chin.

Here is the Stomach that growled for more.
Here are the Legs that ran for the door.

Here are the Ears that heard a whack.
Here is the Bottom that felt a smack!

Clyde Watson

The Mud-pie Makers Rhyme

Mud is squidgy,
slippery, sludgey.
Mud is irmy-squirmy goo.
Mud is runny,
squeezy, funny.
Mud is oozey-woozey too.

Mud you can roll flat,
mud you can press.
Mud is the nicest, muddiest mess.
Mud you can make with,
mud you can share.
Our mud-pies are the best anywhere.

Mud is squidgy,
slippery, sludgey.
Mud is irmy-squirmy goo.
Mud is runny,
squeezy, funny.
Mud is oozey-woozey too.

Janet Paisley

Mud

Take a bucket of soil.
Some water from a can.
Mix them well
in an old saucepan.
Add a few leaves.
Some flowerpetals too.
And soon you'll have
A Mudpie stew.

Take slugs and snails,
a scattering of sand.
Rub them round
with your muddy hand.
Leave in the sun
a while to bake.
And soon you'll have
a Mudpie cake.

Ann Bonner

Plasticine

Here's a piece of plasticine,
All hard and cold.
First of all it has to be
Squeezed and squashed and rolled.

Can you make a big long sausage?
Roll it just like that.
Can you make a little ball,
Nice and round and fat?

Now what shall we make with it?
A man? A flower? A hen?
If it isn't any good,
We'll squash it up again.

Wendy Cope

46

My Old Guitar

I like to play my old guitar,
Strum, strum, strum —
Sometimes with my fingers,
Sometimes with my thumb.

I like to sit around and sing,
And dream that I'm a star.
I like to sit and sing and dream
And play my old guitar.

Wendy Cope

My Bike

I never make a fuss
On a bus.
I never am a pain
On a train
Or a plane.

I never set the goat
Afloat
In a boat.

I never go too far
In a car.

I like
My bike.

John Kitching

Magic Shoes

I've got a pair of magic shoes
they take me to the moon.
Dad says, 'Watch out for the rockets,'
and Mum says, 'Come back soon.'

I've got a pair of magic shoes
they take me to the stars,
and sometimes if I'm early,
I'll stop for tea on Mars.

I've got a pair of magic shoes
I can jump as high as a school,
I can walk up walls like Spiderman
and act like I'm really cool.

I've got a pair of magic shoes
I can dance like a disco king,
they spring me up to the rooftops,
they let me do anything.

But what if I had some magic socks,
some magic underwear too!
With a magic suit of clothes
there's nothing I couldn't do.

Brian Moses

Magic Horse

Black horse,
Magic horse,
Carry me away,
Over the river,
Across the bay
To the sandy beach
Where I can play.

Black horse,
Magic horse,
Carry me away,
Over the seas
To the forest trees
Where I can watch
The tiger cubs play.

Black horse,
Magic horse,
Carry me away
To Arctic snows
Where the cold wind blows
Where I can watch
The polar bears play.

Black horse,
Magic horse
Carry me away
To golden sands
In far-away lands
Where the sea is blue
And I can play all day.

John Foster

this is the key to the castle

this is the key to the castle

this is the box
with rusty locks
that holds the key to the castle

this is the spider, huge and fat,
who wove her web and sat and sat
on top of the box
with rusty locks
that holds the key to the castle

this is the cellar, cold and bare,
dark as a grave, with nothing there
except the spider, huge and fat,
who wove her web and sat and sat
on top of the box
with rusty locks
that holds the key to the castle

this is the stair that rumbles and creaks
where every small step moans and squeaks,
that leads to the cellar, cold and bare,
dark as the grave, with nobody there
except the spider, huge and fat
who wove her web and sat and sat
on top of the box
with rusty locks
that holds the key to the castle

this is the rat with yellow teeth,
sharp as sorrow and long as grief,
who ran up the creaking crumbling stair,
up from the cellar, cold and bare,
dark as the grave, with nobody there
except the spider, huge and fat,
who wove her web and sat and sat
on top of the box
with rusty locks
that holds the key to the castle

this is the damp and dirty hall
with peeling paper on its mouldy wall
where the black rat runs with yellow teeth
sharp as sorrow and long as grief
at the top of the stair that crumbles and creaks
where every small step moans and squeaks,
that leads up from the cellar, cold and bare,
dark as a grave, with nobody there
except the spider, huge and fat,
who wove her web and sat and sat
on top of the box
with rusty locks
that holds the key to the castle

this is the ghost with rattling bones
carrying his head, whose horrible groans
fill the damp and dirty hall
with peeling paper on its mouldy wall
where the big black rat with yellow teeth
sharp as sorrow, long as grief,
runs to the stair that crumbles and creaks
where every small step moans and squeaks
that leads to the cellar, cold and bare
and dark as a grave with nobody there
except the spider, huge and fat,
who wove her web and sat and sat
on top of the box
with rusty locks

54

this is the child who came to play
on a rainy, windy, nasty day

and said BOO to the ghost who groaned in the hall
and SCAT to the rat by the mouldy wall
and went down the creaking crumbling stair
into the cellar, cold and bare,
and laughed at the spider, huge and fat,
and brushed off the web where it sat and sat
and opened the box
with the rusty locks
and took the key to the castle

Dave Calder

Jungle Wedding

When the hairy hippopotamus
And dapper duck-billed platypus
Decided to get married in the spring,
All the jungle bells were ringing
And the tree-top choirs were singing,
But they couldn't find a shop to buy a ring.

Clive Webster

The Fiery Dragon

Oh, the fiery, fiery dragon
Blows fire out through his nose.
But oh, he takes great care, great care,
In case he burns his toes.

Clive Webster

A Big Bare Bear

A big bare bear
           bought a bear balloon,
For a big bear trip
           to the bare, bare moon.
A hairy bear
           saw the bare bear fly
On the big bear trip
           in the bare, bare sky.
The hairy bear
           took a jet up high
To catch the bear
           in the big bare sky.
The hairy bear
           flew his jet right by
The bear balloon
           in the big bare sky.
He popped the balloon
           with his hairy thumb,
And the bare bear fell
           on his big bum bum.

Robert Heidbreder

The Underwater Camel

The underwater camel
Lives in streams and lakes and pools,
His hobbies are collecting stamps
And jumping over stools.

He likes to wear pyjamas
And play the slide trombone,
And if you ring his number
He'll play it down the 'phone.

Jonathan Allen

Roger was a Razor Fish

Roger was a razor fish
as sharp as he could be.
He said to Calvin Catfish
'I'll shave you for a fee.'

'No thanks,'
said Calvin Catfish.
'I like me like I be.'
And with his whiskers
on his face
he headed out to sea.

Al Pittman

The Picallili Monster

Who's that coming
Walking down the street?
It's the Picallili Monster
With his big green feet.
It's the Picallili Monster
With his cauliflower nose
And his big yellow body
And his little green toes.

Oh, the Picallili Monster
Is a very friendly chap
And he'll sit all day
With lots of children in his lap.
And it doesn't really matter
If they get a little yellow
For the Picallili Monster
Is such a jolly fellow.

David Andrews

A Garden

If I should have a garden
I know how it would be,
There'd be daisies and buttercups
And an apple tree.

A dog would chase a ball there,
A bird would sit and sing,
And a little cat would play with
A little piece of string.

And in the very middle
I'd only have to stand
For ladybirds and butterflies
To settle on my hand.

Leila Berg

Swinging

Swinging, swinging,
Low and high,
Down in the green grass
And up in the sky.
When I'm bigger I'll stand when I swing,
When I'm bigger I'll do everything.

Swinging, swinging,
Low and high,
Up in the tree-tops
Down by and by.
When I'm bigger, then I can try,
When I'm bigger I'll reach to the sky.

Swinging, swinging,
High and low,
Up to the sun
And down I go.

Leila Berg

Over the park

I want to go on the see-saw,
I want to go on the slide
and, look, over there is the roundabout . . .
I want to have a ride.

I know I've been on the see-saw,
I know I've been on the slide,
I know I've been on the roundabout,
I know I've had a ride.

I know we've been here a long time
and I've fallen off the see-saw,
I know I've had lots and lots of goes,
but can't I have one more?
Pleeeeeeeeeeeese . . .

Charles Thomson

Like an Animal

I snarl and snap
around the park
pretend that I'm a
strong fierce shark

I jump and hop
off a fallen log
pretend that I'm a
bright-eyed frog

I slide zig-zag
beside the lake
pretend that I'm a
patterned snake

I leap and spring
bound
everywhere
pretend that I'm a
long-legged hare

Joan Poulson

Gone

I had it today
For just an hour,
Then, tugged away
By the wind's power
It sailed off free
Above the crowd,
High as a tree,
High as a cloud,
High as the moon,
High as the sun,
My blue balloon
Has gone, gone, gone.

Eric Finney

65

Fancy Me

A wee creepy crawly
crawled and creeped
along the leafie through.
He splished and splashed
past dibbly drops
of wishy washy dew.
And down the bendy bough
he chomped,
champing willy-nilly.
Until he felt
his tummyfull
was gurgling giggly-silly.

Worry me, he cried
and curled
into a safely spot.
And snoozing soft,
he slept and slept
snizzling quite a lot.

66

The winkly sun
tickled his tum
and woke him up to see
wings and things
and traily bits
bobbling round him free.

He stretched and fell
into the sky,
a flittering, floating
butterfly
who didn't think
of quizzling why
but just said,
Fancy me.

Janet Paisley

Tadpoles

Ten little tadpoles
    playing in a pool,
'Come,' said the water-rat,
    'come along to school.
Come and say your tables,
    sitting in a row.'
And all the little tadpoles said,
    'No, no, no!'

Ten little tadpoles
    swimming in and out,
Racing and diving
    and turning round about.
'Come,' said their mother,
    'dinner-time, I guess.'
And all the little tadpoles cried,
    'Yes, yes, yes!'

Rose Fyleman

My Friend Camilla

Before the winter
my friend Camilla
was a squiggly wriggly
caterpillar.

But soon she changed
her name to Chris
and turned into
a chrysalis.

In the spring she said,
'My name is Di,'
and then became
a butterfly!

Charles Thomson

Caribbean Counting Rhyme

One by one
one by one
waves are dancing
in the sun.

Two by two
two by two
seashells pink
and purply-blue.

Three by three
three by three
big boats
putting out to sea.

Four by four
four by four
children fishing
on the shore.

Five by five
five by five
little walking
fish arrive.

Six by six
six by six
pelicans
performing tricks.

Seven by seven
seven by seven
puffy clouds
patrolling heaven.

Eight by eight
eight by eight
fishes nibbling
juicy bait.

Nine by nine
nine by nine
taking home
a catch that's fine.

Ten by ten
ten by ten
tomorrow we
will come again.

Pamela Mordecai

Where are you going, Johnny?

Where are you going Johnny-Just-For-A-Lark?
I'm going to play football down at the park.

Where are you going Johnny-Head-In-The-Air?
To ride on the merry-go-round at the fair.

Where are you going Johnny-Rushing-From-School?
I'm going for a swim in the swimming pool.

Where are you going Johnny-Licking-Your-Lips?
I'm off to the fish shop to buy fish and chips.

Where are you going Johnny-Looking-So-Glum?
I'm going into town to go shopping with Mum.

John Foster

Come-day Go-day

Here comes Monday.
School has begun day.
It's a hit-and-run day.
What a very glum day.
There goes Monday.

Here comes Tuesday.
Chase away the blues day.
You can pick and choose day.
Let's have a snooze day.
There goes Tuesday.

Here comes Wednesday.
Tying up the ends day.
It's a let's pretends day.
Drive you round the bends day.
There goes Wednesday.

Here comes Thursday.
It's a his and hers day.
Seen and not heard day.
Quite a connoisseur's day.
There goes Thursday.

Friday

Here comes Friday.
Knocks you sky-high day.
Sing a lullaby day.
Get some shuteye day.
There goes Friday.

Saturday

Here comes Saturday.
Let's have a natter day.
Run and scatter day.
Mad as a hatter day.
There goes Saturday.

Sunday

Here comes Sunday.
Meat overdone day.
Let's have some fun day.
Forget about Monday.
There goes Sunday.

Barrie Wade

The Sunshine Tree

If I had just one wish to wish
Do you know what it would be?
That growing in my garden
Was a great big sunshine tree.

A tree that never rained or blew,
A tree that shone all day.
And there I'd sit with all my toys
And play and play and play.

Clive Webster

76

The Farmer's Shadow

Soft is the farmer's shadow
Upon the golden corn,
As we set off a-harvesting
In the early morn.

Swift is the farmer's shadow
When work is to be done.
The straw we bundle into sheaves
In the midday sun.
Long is the farmer's shadow
As we all make our way
Along the path that takes us home
At the end of day.

Colin West

Clouds

Little bits of cloud
High in the sky,
Little bits of cloud
Float slowly by,
Count all the bits
And that will be,
The number of fishes
There are in the sea.

Valerie Bloom

A Dibble-dubble Day

it's wet
dibble-dubble
it's wet
piddle-puddle
it's rained the
whole day long

the roof-top gutters
and the window shutters
splish-splosh
with the raindrops song —

'pitter-patter
potter-putter
split! splat! splot!

spitter-spatter
splotter-splutter
splish! splash! splosh!'

Joan Poulson

When the Wind Blows

When the wind blows
Coats flap, scarves flutter.

When the wind blows
Branches groan, leaves mutter.

When the wind blows
Curtains swish, papers scatter.

When the wind blows
Gates creak, dustbins clatter.

When the wind blows
Doors slam, windows rattle.

When the wind blows
Inside is a haven,
Outside is a battle.

John Foster

Storm

Jagged light, blue and bright
Flashes in the air
Rumble bumble, crash boom
What's going on up there?

The Man in the Moon is having a party
Fireworks burst and fly
As wild drums and dancing feet
Echo through the sky.

Clyde Watson

Giant Thunderclogs

Here comes Giant
    Thunderclogs!
What a noise
    he makes!
How he rattles, rants
    and roars,
how he shouts
    and shakes!

Blundering
    across the hills
and stamping
    through the sky . . .
what a tantrum
    he is in
as he passes
    by!

Giant Thunderclogs
     is huge . . .
his mouth
     is like a pit
and all the echoes
     of the earth
come rushing out
     of it:

Not fifty thousand
     elephants
could trumpet
     such a din.
If you hear him
     at your gate . . .

Don't let him in!

Jean Kenward

Snow-lady

Snow-lady, snow-lady,
Out there in the cold
With your fat carrot-nose
And your buttons of gold;
The hat on your head
Has a snow-ribbon band
And a robin has perched
On your ice-stiffened hand.

Snow-lady, snow-lady
Please don't go away!
We'll build a tall snowman
Beside you today.
Then you won't feel lonely
Out there in the night,
With the moon shining down
And the frosty starlight.

Mary Jefferies

The Snowstorm

Heave-ho,
Buckets of snow,
The giant is combing his beard.
The snow is as high
As the top of the sky,
And the world has disappeared.

Dennis Lee

Jack Frost

He creeps through the grass,
Catch as catch can,
Cold in his fingers,
A slippery man.

Magic his cloak of
Snowflake lace,
He steals away warmth
And leaves ice in its place.

Theresa Heine

Ice

When it is the winter time
I run up the street
And I make the ice laugh
With my little feet —
'Crickle, crackle, crickle
Crreet, crrreeet, crrreeet.'

Dorothy Aldis

Polar Bear

Polar bear, polar bear,
How do you keep clean?
You always seem to stay so white
No matter where you've been.

My mummy scrubs me every night
To wash the dirt away.
Somehow it all comes back again
When I go out to play.

Polar bear, polar bear,
Do you ever bath?
I seem to get so dirty
Just walking up the path.

I wish I was a polar bear,
So then every night
If someone tries to bath me
I'd growl at them and bite!

Spike Milligan

Bath-time

Daddy turn the taps on,
Let the water in,
I'm a fishy in the sea,
A fishy with a great big fin.

Mummy make the bubbles,
When the water's in,
I'll be Father Christmas
With a beard upon my chin.

Daddy pull the boats along,
Now the water's in,
I'm the captain on the bridge,
In charge of everything.

Mummy take me out now,
Leave the water in,
I'll be a slippery porpoise
With a clean and shiny skin.

Tony Bradman

Sitting in my Bath-tub

Sitting in my bath-tub,
I have sailed the seven seas.
I have anchored by the taps.
I've been shipwrecked off the knees.

I have sailed into the unknown
To beat off an attack
From a fleet of pirates lurking
Round behind my back.

I have sailed between the fingers
Where no other ship has been.
I've explored the murky depths
In a soapy submarine.

Sitting in my bath-tub,
I have sailed the seven seas.
I have anchored by the taps.
I've been shipwrecked off the knees.

John Foster

After a Bath

After my bath
I try, try, try
to wipe myself
till I'm dry, dry, dry.

Hands to wipe
and fingers and toes
and two wet legs
and a shiny nose.

Just think how much
less time I'd take
if I were a dog
and could shake, shake, shake.

Aileen Fisher

Water Everywhere

There's water on the ceiling,
And water on the wall,
There's water in the bedroom,
And water in the hall,
There's water on the landing,
And water on the stair,
Whenever Daddy takes a bath
There's water everywhere.

Valerie Bloom

91

Hair Drier

My mum's hair drier
buzzes like a bee
Looks like a ray gun
when she points it at me.

'Into the bath now,
to shampoo your hair,
then out for a rub down
and a blow of hot air.'

It prickles my head
and tingles my ears,
It tickles my neck
as it zooms and it whirrs.

It whizzes and whooshes
and buzzes at me
It sounds much more like
a bad-tempered bee!

Maggie Holmes

Bed-time

Bed-time, bed-time,
Hot milk, honeyed-bread time,
Favourite book to read time,
Best rhymes to be said time,
Stairs quietly tread time,
Cosy bedspread time,
Cuddle with Ted time,
Eyes heavy as lead time,
Sleepy old head time.
Bed-time, bed-time.

John Kitching

Patchy Bear

I'm a roly-poly
plump teddy bear
with a lopsided smile
and gold-coloured fur

I've lost my growl
and a lot of my hair
I'm old and I'm bald
and my fur has gone bare

but I love to be cuddled
and snuggle in bed
I need someone to say
You're my very best Ted

I like listening to stories
to dance and to play
I can keep secrets
and I'll do what you say

I need someone special
a friend just like you
so take care of me
and I'll take care of you.

Joan Poulson

Lullaby

Hush, can you hear
in the thickening deep
the air in the trees
is falling asleep?

Hush, can you see
where the darkening skies
stretch over the sunset
and close heavy eyes?

Hush, can you hear
where the whispering corn
is settling down
and starting to yawn?

Hush, can you see
in the moon's silver beam
the light of the world
beginning to dream?

Hush, can you feel
the whole world give a sigh
and fall fast asleep
to your lullaby?

Barrie Wade

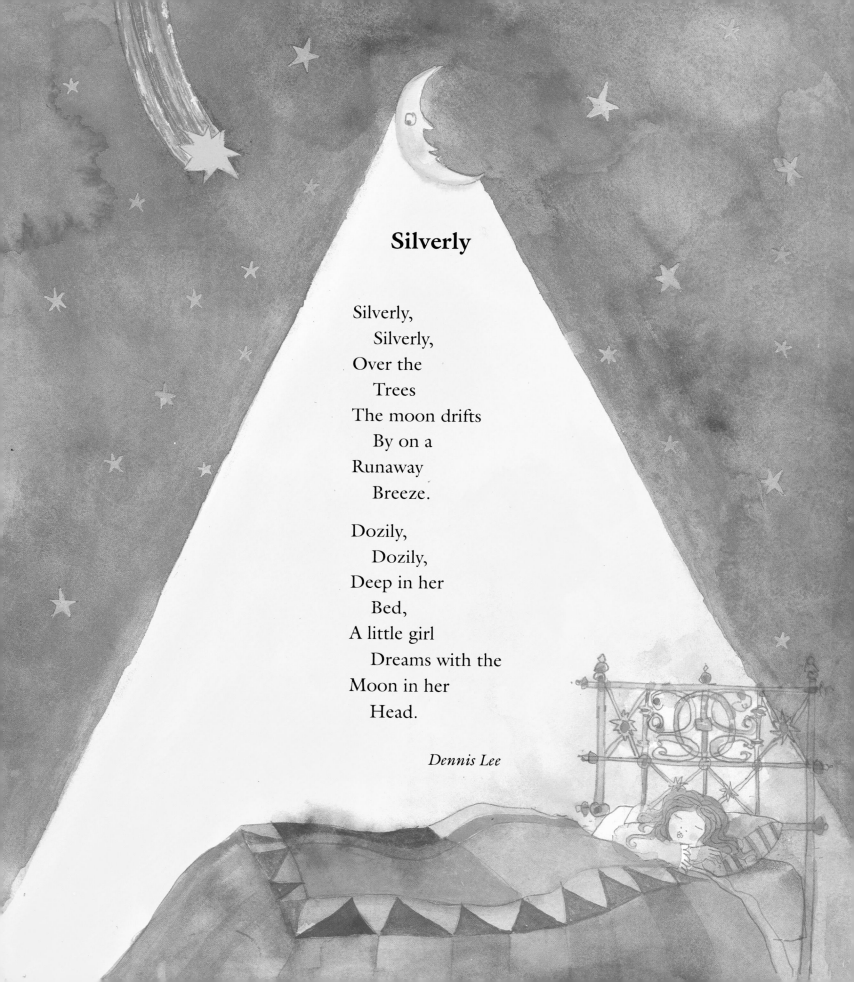

Silverly

Silverly,
Silverly,
Over the
Trees
The moon drifts
By on a
Runaway
Breeze.

Dozily,
Dozily,
Deep in her
Bed,
A little girl
Dreams with the
Moon in her
Head.

Dennis Lee

Where's Melissa?

Melissa dreamed that she could fly
Like a bird-girl in the sky,
She took with her a diamond spoon
To eat the cherry-pancake moon.

David R. Morgan

How Far

'How far away
Is the evening star?'
'Ask the night horse,
He knows how far.

Talk to him gently.
Give him honey and hay,
Seven bells for his bridle
And he'll take you away.

Snorting white fire
He will stream through the air
Past mountains of the moon
And the rainbow's stair.

And if you go singing
Through the dark and the cold
Your purse will be filled
With silver and gold.'

Olive Dove

The Moon

The moon is just a big potato floating in the sky
And little men from outer space are often passing by.
If they're feeling hungry they eat just a bit for dinner,
That's why the moon is sometimes fat,
but at other times it's thinner.

Kjartan Poskitt

Good Night, Good Night

The dark is dreaming.
  Day is done.
Good night, good night
  To everyone.

Good night to the birds,
  And the fish in the sea,
Good night to the bears
  And good night to me.

Dennis Lee

Index of first lines and titles

Titles are shown in *italic*

Going to Sleep

Going to sleep is a funny thing,
I lie in bed and I'm yawning
and Dad is reading a story and then . . .

Suddenly it's morning!

Ian McMillan